Nearly Seamless

Cuffed Bootie Slippers

for Adults

by

Janis Frank

Page 2

Page 6

Table of Contents

If you've run across any of my slipper patterns before this, one thing you'll be very familiar with is my unreasonable dislike for sewing seams on projects. I equally dislike working in ends (go to <u>Hints and Tips</u> section for more on this). I have a embarrassing amount of nearly finished projects that collect in a box with unsewn seams and dangling ends. Yes. I just admitted that to everyone. No shame in my game.

This is another attempt to make this happen. It's quite difficult to make something seamless when the design calls for it to be knit flat on 2 needles. This automatically means there are going to be ends that need to meet at some point. The idea is to make them meet as you knit so they are permanently fixed together with no extra work.

This pattern starts with the cast on stitches going around the foot (*sans* heel). You'll then work your way up to the top cuff. I've pointed out where we're starting in this photo.

Arrows point to the cast on edge

Now that I've figured out how to do this, I have a few other designs I want to develop that take advantage of this method of slipper design.

Things You Need

Worsted weight yarn – 2 (two) standard balls of yarn (215 yards/197 m). Any colours of your choosing.

or

Super Bulky yarn – 2 standard balls of **ONE** colour with matching lot numbers (90 yards/82 m).

One ball makes one slipper. There will be some yarn left over from each ball.

Size 5 mm (size 8 US) knitting needles (or whatever you require to get the correct gauge).

Tapestry needle to sew the seam and work in the ends.

Gauge

In stockinette stitch

8 sts – 5 cm (2")

7 rows – 5 cm (2")

Sizes are written as such:

Women 6-7 (**8-9,** 10-11, **12**)

Men 6 (**7-8,** 9-10, **11-12**)

Cast on 56 (**60,** 64, **68**)

Knit across for 6 (**6,** 8, **8**) rows.

Next Row: K26 (**28,** 30, **32**) K2tog. Sl 1 as if to knit. K1 PSSO. K26 (**28,** 30, **32**).

Next Row: P25 (**27,** 29, **31**) P2tog TBL. P2tog. P25 (**27,** 29, **31**).

Next Row: K24 (**26,** 28, **30**) K2tog. Sl 1 as if to knit. K1 PSSO. K24 (**26,** 28, **30**).

Next Row: P23 (**25,** 27, **29**) P2tog TBL. P2tog. P23 (**25,** 27, **29**).

Next Row: K22 (**24,** 26, **28**) K2tog. Sl 1 as if to knit. K1 PSSO. K22 (**24,** 26, **28**).

Next Row: P21 (**23,** 25, **27**) P2tog TBL. P2tog. P21 (**23,** 25, **27**).

Next Row: K20 (**22,** 24, **26**) K2tog. Sl 1 as if to knit. K1 PSSO. K20 (**22,** 24, **26**).

Next Row: P19 (**21,** 23, **25**) P2tog TBL. P2tog. P19 (**21,** 23, **25**).

Next Row: K18 (**20,** 22, **24**) K2tog. Sl 1 as if to knit. K1 PSSO. K18 (**20,** 22, **24**).

Next Row: P17 (**19,** 21, **23**) P2tog TBL. P2tog. P17 (**19,** 21, **23**).

Next Row: K16 (**18,** 20, **22**) K2tog. Sl 1 as if to knit. K1 PSSO. K16 (**18,** 20, **22**).

Next Row: P15 (**17,** 19, **21**) P2tog TBL. P2tog. P15 (**17,** 19, **21**).

Next Row: K14 (**16,** 18, **20**) K2tog. Sl 1 as if to knit. K1 PSSO. K14 (**16,** 18, **20**).

Next Row: P13 (**15,** 17, **19**) P2tog TBL. P2tog. P13 (**15,** 17, **19**). If making women's size 6-7 or men's size 6, go to the row marked with ☺ .

*Next Row: K4 M1. K0 (**10,** 12, **14**). K2tog. Sl 1 as if to knit. K1 PSSO. K0 (**10,** 12, **14**). M1 K4.

Next Row: P2 PM1. P0 (**12,** 14, **16**). P2tog TBL. P2tog. P0 (**12,** 14, **16**). PM1 P2.*
Repeat from * to * 0 (**1,** 2, **3**) times *more*.

☺ Knit across for 6 (**6,** 8, **8**) rows.

Cast off *loosely*.

Making the Sole

This photo will help you in how and where to pick up the following stitches. Hold your work so it looks like this with the pointy end up. The RED arrow is for right handed knitters.

Pick up 6 sts at the toe in bottom loop of cast on stitches. (3 sts on either side of middle clearly marked with p2tog line.)

Next Row: Knit across.

Next Row: Pick up a stitch in the bottom loop of the cast on stitches. K6. Pick up a stitch in the bottom loop of the cast on stitches.

Next Row: Knit across.

Next Row: Pick up a stitch in the bottom loop of the cast on stitches. K8. Pick up a stitch in the bottom loop of the cast on stitches.

Next Row: Knit across.

If you are making women's sizes 6-9 or men's sizes 6-8, skip to row marked with ♥

For all other sizes continue as follows:

Next Row: Pick up a stitch in the bottom loop of the cast on stitches. K10. Pick up a stitch in the bottom loop of the cast on stitches.

Next Row: Knit across.

♥ ☼ Next Row: Pick up a stitch in the bottom loop of the cast on stitches. K2tog. Knit to last 2 sts. K2tog. Pick up a stitch in the bottom loop of the cast on stitches.

Next Row: Knit across. ☼

Repeat rows marked with ☼ to ☼ down the length of the sole. You will ALWAYS have 10 (**10**, 12, **12**) sts on your needle.

Take a photo of this square for
FREE knitting pattens on my website!

Forming the Heel

There are two ways to do this. The easiest way is to *make a small triangle*.

Using the 10 (**10**, 12, **12**) sts on your needle.

♦ Next **2** Rows: Knit across.

Next Row: K2tog. Knit to last 2 sts. K2tog.

Next Row: Knit across. ♦
Repeat from ♦ to ♦ until 5 (**5,** 6, **6**) sts

If making women's sizes 6-9 or men's sizes 6-8:

Next Row: K2tog K1 K2tog.

Next Row: K3tog. Cut yarn and draw yarn through last st. Leave a length of yarn long enough to sew the remaining seam.

If making women's sizes 10-12 or men's sizes 9-12:

Next Row: K2tog 3 times.

Next Row: K3tog. Cut yarn and draw yarn through last st. Leave a length of yarn long enough to sew the remaining seam.

For all sizes:
Flip up the triangle to fit into the back of the heel. Sew seams along sides of triangle and up the back of the slipper.

Or

Make the seams as you go:

Using the 10 (**10**, 12, **12**) sts on your needle,
♦ Next Row: Pick up a st along side of the slipper. K2tog twice. Knit to last 4 sts. K2tog twice. Pick up a st along side of the slipper and work in the ends.

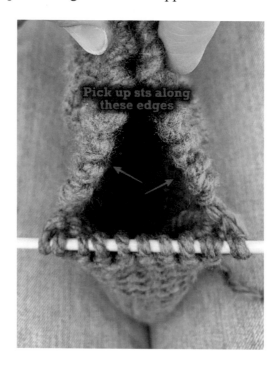

Next Row: Knit across. ♦

Repeat from ♦ to ♦ until 6 (**6**, 8, **8**) sts.

§ Next Row: Pick up a st along side of the slipper. K2tog across. Pick up a st along side of the slipper.

Next Row: Knit across. §

If making women's sizes 10-12 or men's sizes 9-12, repeat from § to § *once.*

Next Row: Pick up a st along side of the slipper. K2tog, K1, K2tog. Pick up a st along side of the slipper.

Next Row: K2tog, K1, K2tog.

Next Row: K3tog. Cut yarn and draw yarn through last st. Leave a length of yarn long enough to sew the remaining seam. Sew the seam up the back of the slipper and work in the ends.

Hints and Tips

You can make the slippers truly seamless when you are making the seamed triangle for the back of the heel. Continue picking up stitches on each side while working up the heel seam. Continue doing this using the 5 sts and repeating as follows:

Next Row: Pick up a st along side of the slipper. K2tog, K1, K2tog. Pick up a st along side of the slipper.

Next Row: Knit across.

I didn't include it in the instructions because... I didn't. It was already complicated enough for the heel.

If you are up in arms about how many ends there are to sew in, you can work the ends in while you are knitting. I have a detailed photo tutorial on my website here that you can watch – How to Work In the Ends While Knitting at this link https://bit.ly/knitends or you can take a photo of this QR code

Play around with the colours you choose if you're using worsted weight yarn. You can get some neat effects by blending a solid colour with a variegated one, or by using colours that are the same colour but a different tone. I used both of these techniques for the red booties.

Abbreviations

st - stitch

sts – stitches

sl – slip the stitch

PSSO – pass slipped stitch over.

K - knit

P - purl

PM1 – Make one (purl wise). Increase one stitch between the stitches. Pick up the yarn between the stitches. Twist it slightly and place it on your non-working needle. Purl the stitch. Watch this video on **How to PM1 or Purl Make 1** to see how.

M1 – Make one (knit wise). Increase one stitch between the stitches. Pick up the yarn between the stitches. Twist it slightly and place it on your non-working needle. Knit the stitch. Watch this video on **How to M1 or Make 1** to see how.

K2tog - knit 2 stitches together

K3tog – knit 3 stitches together

P2tog - purl 2 stitches together

P2tog TBL - purl 2 together through the back loop. (Photos on next page).

Yarn Over (YO) and pull through.

Like all of my patterns you have my permission to sell and/or give away the physical items that you make using this pattern. You are NOT permitted to reprint or duplicate this pattern in any form unless you have obtained my written permission to do so.

If you have any questions, please feel free to leave a comment or send me your questions at kweenbee_crafts@hotmail.ca.

Help Support My Work!

Follow me on Tik Tok, Instagram, Twitter, Facebook, Pinterest and YouTube. Every follow, subscribe, thumbs up, like, heart and share help increase my popularity on the web and get more viewers to my work. It costs you nothing but helps me sooooo much!

If you would like to help a little more, you can always support me on Patreon or you can make a single time donation at Buy Me a Coffee.

More FREE knitting patterns on my website

This is the latest list of patterns I have on my website. It is an ever growing list so you might want to This is the latest list of patterns I have on my website. It is an ever growing list so you might want to check out my **Free Knitting Patterns** page at **KweenBee.com** . I design new patterns as I get time and add them to my website.

To make it even easier, you can take a photo of the QR code below with your phone or tablet. It will take you right to the webpage!

If you would like to access any of the patterns you can easily do an internet search to find them. When you are on your favourite search engine like Google, Bing, Yahoo, etc. Enter the term ***Kweenbee*** and the title as it is written below (capitalization isn't important). It will pop up for you in the search results and be super-easy to find.

For example, enter it like this:

Q   kweenbee Diamonds Dishcloth   ✕

Google Search   I'm Feeling Lucky

Google offered in: Français

Your results will have my pattern at the very top...usually. Depending on the popularity of the pattern, you may get a link to Pinterest or Ravelry first. Don't worry! All of those options have links back to my original patterns, too!

Easy to Knit Beginner Slipper Pattern - Knit Flat with Bulky Yarn on Straight Needles

How to Knit Spider Fingerless Gloves - Knit Flat on 2 Needles

Winter Beanie Toque or Touque or Tuque with Vertical Stripes

Minimalist Round Toe Slippers – Knit Flat on 2 Needles

One Piece Knitted Dishcloth and Coasters

Knitting for Beginners – Knit a Dishcloth

Easy to Knit Long Cuffed Slippers

Easy to Knit Rolled Cuff Slippers

Knit a Pair of Texting Mitts

Chevron Striped Moccasin Slippers

Super Cozy Textured Adult Bootie Slippers

Textured Easy to Knit Dishcloth Pattern

Super Simple Fingerless Gloves – Knit Flat on 2 Needles

Easy to Knit **OWL** Fingerless Gloves – Knit Flat on 2 Needles

Knit Long Fingerless Gloves – Two Styles with One Pattern

Super Simple Knit Slippers

Cable Fingerless Gloves

How to Knit Fingerless Arm Warmers or Mitts – with Bows!

How to Knit Fingerless Gloves

Bars and Stripes Knitted Dishcloth Pattern

How to Knit Fingerless Gloves – with OWLS!

FREE Knitted Slipper Pattern for Children

FREE Knitted Slipper Pattern for Adults

How to Knit Adult Slippers

How to Knit Ribbed Bootie Slippers for Adults

Adorable Sheep Slippers

Diamonds Dishcloth

Cute AF Bows Dishcloth – FREE Knitting Pattern

How to Knit Slippers Like Granny Made

Knit Two Styles of Slippers with One Pattern

Adult & Child Knitted Slippers…With BOWS!!

Easy to Knit Slippers – Great Beginner Knitting Pattern

Cable Knit Slippers for Children and Adults

How to Knit Socks & Graft a Toe – With Photos

Cable Knit Wine Bottle Cozy or Koozie

Knit a Simple Dishcloth

How to Knit a Way Cool Monster Purse

How to Knit a Cable Scarf aka Netflix and Knit…This Scarf

How to Knit a Pair of Flip Mittens or Fingerless Gloves

How to Knit Adult Bootie Slippers

How to Knit Children's Slippers – Free Knitting Pattern

Knitted Adult Slippers with a Plaid Pattern

Follow Me on Social Media

Me on Pinterest - http://www.pinterest.com/kweenbee_crafts

Like Me on Facebook - https://www.facebook.com/janis.the.knitter/

Me on YouTube - https://www.youtube.com/user/KweenBeeCrafts

Instagram - https://www.instagram.com/janis_as_in_joplin

Twitter - https://twitter.com/Crafty_Janis

KweenBee.com

My Etsy Shop - http://www.etsy.com/shop/KweenBee

Become a Patron on Patreon! - https://www.patreon.com/JanisFrank

Buy Me a Coffee - https://www.buymeacoffee.com/JanisFrank

Notes